GO AHEAD
LAUGH!

COLLECTED BRIDGE HUMOR OF JUDE GOODWIN

MASTER POINT PRESS | TORONTO

Master Point Press
331 Douglas Ave.
Toronto, Ontario, Canada
M5M 1H2
(416) 781-0351
Website: http://www.masterpointpress.com
Email: info@masterpointpress.com

Library and Archives Canada Cataloguing in Publication

Goodwin, Jude

Go ahead, laugh! : collected bridge humor of Jude Goodwin / written and illustrated by Jude Goodwin.

ISBN-10 1-897106-16-5
ISBN-13 978-1-897106-16-7

1. Contract bridge--Humor. I. Title.

GV1282.32.G66 2006   795.41'50207   C2006-
904819-3

Editor   Ray Lee
Interior format and copy editing   Suzanne Hocking
Cover and interior design   Olena S. Sullivan/New Mediatrix

We acknowledge the financial support of the Government of Canada through the Book Publishing Industry Development Program (BPIDP) for our publishing activities.

Printed in Canada by Webcom Inc.

1 2 3 4 5 6 7   10 09 08 07 06

FOREW☺RD

Years ago, as young women in our twenties, my friend Julie Smith and I began what would be a wonderful sojourn into the world of tournament bridge. For almost a decade we traveled around British Columbia, Washington and Alberta, attending every sectional we could. Julie worked full time as a teacher and I was the mother of two young daughters, but beyond those priorities, we devoted every waking moment to our new-found passion.

The cartoons in this book are, for the most part, based on our experiences during those years. In the late 70s, after the kids were in bed, I would escape to my studio to work on perfecting a cartooning technique. Would my characters have big heads or little? Should I do strips or cells? And how does one draw chairs around a bridge table anyhow? Finally, I had enough drafts to seek a publisher. In 1982, Randy Baron of Devyn Press agreed to publish a book of strips which I called *Table Talk*.

There was only ever one print run of the book, but I'll never forget the day I held it in my hands and realized that anything was possible, even a book of cartoons where the characters play cards sitting in mid-air.

Over the years, I continued to work on my technique. I switched to a single cell format; I learned how to draw chairs; then I learned how to draw hands. At each stage, upgraded equipment (pens, paper and eventually the computer) let me improve my drawings.

This book is a collection of my favorite cartoons. You will find the first book reprinted almost in its entirety, with no chairs added. You will also find seventy or so single-cell cartoons which I drew between 1982 and 2000. Many of them have appeared in the *ACBL Daily Bulletins*, the *ACBL Bridge Bulletin*, the *Daily Bridge Calendar*, *Better Bridge Magazine*, various books and other regional newsletters and magazines.

I would like to acknowledge the following people and sources for their inspiration: Jim Unger, Charles Shulz and Gary Larson, whose genius give me not only endless joy but also lots of good ideas; Julie Smith, Don Ellison, Ian Glover, Joel Martineau, Phil Wood and the many other real people who gave my characters such great personalities; the *ACBL Bridge Bulletin*, which often supplied my punch lines; Henry Francis, for being the first to believe in me; Aidan Ballantyne, for his dry humor and one-liners; and finally, my daughters, Sky and Jewel, who tolerated my many weekends away from home, never complained and were always proud of their mom.

And thank you, dear readers, for all the years of your laughter.

Jude Goodwin

THE EAGER YOUNG PLAYER JUST ENTERING THE ARENA OF BRIDGE MUST CULTIVATE CUNNING AND DISCIPLINE

THE PRIMAL DRUMBEAT OF COMPETITION CAN LURE THE STRONGEST OVER THE PRECIPICE OF INCOMPETENCE

BUT A FEW BRIGHT STARS WILL ACTUALLY RISE ABOVE THE JUNGLE HORIZON TO AMAZE THE THOUSANDS LEFT BEHIND

MOVE OVER RON ANDERSEN

OH DUKE-I'M SUCH A BASKET CASE..I'LL NEVER BE ANY GOOD AT THIS GAME I TRY AND TRY AND LOSE AND LOSE-I'M SO UPSET!

Laugh!

HEY. DID SUE TELL YOU ABOUT THE HAND WHERE SHE MISSED 4TH SUIT FORCING? THAT'S THE SAME HAND WHERE SHE LOST THE ACE OF HEARTS AND...

BAM

THERE ARE ADVANTAGES TO LIVING IN A CARTOON STRIP-A PERSON CAN **DO** THAT SORT OF THING...